THE BASICS OF PERSONAL PROTECTION

A Practical Handgun Handbook

First Edition

Produced by the Safety and Education Division
and the
Recreational Shooting, Training, and Ranges Division

A Publication of the National Rifle Association of America

First Edition—September, 1988

©1988 The National Rifle Association of America

International Standard Book Number (ISBN): 0-935998-71-3

ES5N2061   *11–93*

FOREWORD

The NRA Personal Protection Program is the National Rifle Association's response to thousands of Americans who own handguns for personal protection and desire to learn to use their firearms with even greater safety and skill. This desire affirms the belief that the majority of handgun owners want to exercise their rights to gun ownership and self-protection responsibly.

The NRA believes that one of the fundamental legitimate purposes of our right to possess firearms is to allow a citizen to exercise his or her individual right of self-preservation and defense of family and person. The NRA believes in the dignity of self-defense and the right of all law-abiding persons to own firearms to protect themselves and their families if they so choose.

The decision to buy a handgun or other firearm is a personal decision that must be made only after fully and carefully considering several important questions: Do you have the will to use a firearm in a life-threatening situation? Does any possible risk to your personal safety justify this decision? How would the use of a firearm for self-protection affect other persons in your family or home?

For those who decide to defend themselves, the NRA Personal Protection Program provides the basic knowledge to operate and use a handgun safely and to teach the fundamentals needed to shoot it skillfully. Of course, mastery of those skills can come only with practice.

Every aspect of this program has been developed and tested by experts in law, law enforcement, firearms technology and shooting instruction. To master this information, you are encouraged to study this handbook in your home, but, preferably, to take a Personal Protection course from an NRA Certified Instructor. Contact the NRA Training Department, 1600 Rhode

Island Avenue, N.W., Washington, D.C. 20036 for information or a list of local instructors.

The NRA offers this program and this handbook to support your individual right to use a handgun as a means of personal protection. We are confident your participation in this program will better prepare you to exercise that right.

ACKNOWLEDGMENTS

The NRA Personal Protection Handbook was developed by the NRA Safety and Education Division and Recreational Shooting, Training, and Ranges Division with technical assistance from NRA Headquarters offices, including: Executive Staff, Field Services, Law Enforcement Activities, General Counsel, Publications and others.

The National Rifle Association gratefully acknowledges the significant contributions of the following individuals in the development of this handbook and the NRA Personal Protection Program.

Jeanne Bray — Detective, Columbus, Ohio Police Department; nationally recognized authority on personal protection; five-time National Women's Police Revolver champion; member, NRA Board of Directors; member, NRA Women's Policies Committee.

David Caplan, Ph.D. — Attorney, New York, New York; widely published author of articles on the Second Amendment in popular and scholarly media; chief counsel, Federation of New York State Rifle & Pistol Clubs; member, NRA Board of Directors.

Sue W. Caplan — Attorney, New York City; law professor, Baruch College Law Department; assistant counsel, New York State Rifle & Pistol Association; member, NRA Board of Directors; member, NRA Women's Policies Committee.

Marcia Carlson, Ph.D. — Professor, State University of New York at Cortland; author of published articles and research grants on outdoor education; member, NRA Board of Directors; chairman, NRA Women's Policies Committee.

Jim Carmichel — Shooting Editor, *Outdoor Life* magazine; author, "The Women's Guide to Handguns"; served as special White House advisor to the Crime Control Commission; member, NRA Board of Directors.

Lawrence Katz — Constitutional Lawyer, Miami, Florida; lecturer in criminal and international law in the U.S. and Europe; listed in "Who's Who in American Law"; general counsel, U.S. Shooting Team; member, International Shooter Development Fund Board of Directors; member, NRA Legal Action Committee.

John Layton — Chief of Police, Washington, D.C., (retired); past President, NRA; member, U.S. Olympic Pistol Team (1948); member, NRA Executive Council.

Joseph A. Nava — Active NRA Personal Protection Instructor; Executive Officer, Institute of Arctic Biology, University of Alaska; member, NRA Board of Directors.

Dick Newell — Graduate, FBI Academy; former Supervisor of Firearms Training, Los Angeles Police Department.

Ann Otis — President, Bayou Rifle Club, Houston, Texas; member, Board of Directors, Houston Gun Collectors; member, NRA Women's Policies Committee.

Robert Pemberton, Sr. — Detective, Nassau Co., New York Police Department (retired).

Harry Reeves — Police Inspector, Detroit, Michigan (retired); member, U.S. Olympic Pistol Team (1952); six-time National Pistol Champion; member, NRA Board of Directors.

Clyde Sellers — Chief of Police, Tarrant, Alabama (retired); police firearms instructor; referee, police combat competition.

INTRODUCTION

Today, many responsible, law-abiding Americans are buying handguns for one reason: to protect themselves and their families. If you are among them, you know the decision is not an easy one. Most people do not want to consider the possibility of having to defend themselves or their families against a violent criminal attack. At the same time, no one likes to consider the consequences of being helpless and unable to prevent a senseless tragedy.

In a criminally threatening situation, a handgun can be a psychological, as well as a physical, stopping force that can save innocent lives and discourage violence, a fact clearly established statistically. Many Americans feel their handguns may mean the difference between becoming the victim or the victor in a confrontation with a criminal.

But our subject is not crime, nor is it our intention to convince you that obtaining a firearm is the only—or even the best—way to defend yourself against violent criminal acts. That is a decision only you can make.

Our subject is the safe and practical use of handguns. Anyone who buys a handgun for personal protection needs to learn to handle it safely and to maintain reasonable proficiency by regularly practicing shooting fundamentals. That may seem obvious, but some people who choose a handgun for self-protection hope that they will never have to use it and, consequently, do not learn the operation and potential of their gun. Others believe the mere presence of a firearm will be enough to ward off a criminal.

It is true that just showing a handgun may give you control of a situation and that you will never need to pull the trigger. However, a good working knowledge of handguns and shooting safety is essential. Being familiar and comfortable with your handgun gives you confidence in the mechanics of operation and shooting. Thus, if you must use your gun, you will be prepared.

This handbook has been written to provide a practical understanding of handguns and the fundamentals of shooting them. Key objectives are to . . .

1. Teach the rules of safe handling and shooting of handguns.
2. Provide guidelines for selecting handguns and ammunition.
3. Provide general guidelines for safe loading, unloading and firing of handguns.
4. Review procedures for the care and storage of firearms.
5. Teach the fundamentals of handgun marksmanship.
6. Introduce ways to maintain shooting skills.
7. Offer suggestions for avoiding or controlling criminal attack.
8. Highlight federal, state and local laws pertaining to the purchase, ownership, possession and transportation of handguns.

Shooting is a motor control skill. To develop this skill, one learns the fundamentals, preferably in practice sessions supervised by NRA Certified Instructors. These knowledgeable individuals have demonstrated the qualifications to teach firearm skills to others. NRA Personal Protection Courses are offered throughout the country. Through demonstrations, discussions and practical training sessions, NRA Instructors provide basic instruction for those who have acquired or who plan to acquire a handgun for personal protection.

While self-study of this handbook will greatly aid your understanding of handguns, we encourage you to attend an NRA Personal Protection Course to become a more confident and knowledgeable gunowner.

CONTENTS

CAUTION: The handbook and program are designed only to teach students basic firearm safety and basic handgun operation. This program does not teach tactics or the use of deadly force and its legal aspects.

PART ONE:

KNOWING YOUR HANDGUN

N R A

PERSONAL
PROTECTION
P R O G R A M

1. HANDGUN PARTS

The responsibility you must accept each time you handle your handgun is fundamental. A handgun is a mechanical device and, as with other machines, you must know how the equipment works before you can master it and use it safely. In the hands of a safety conscious person familiar with its operation, a handgun is safe and reliable. Familiarity with your handgun is the first step in knowing how to shoot safely.

Revolvers and semiautomatics are two types of handguns most commonly chosen for personal protection. Although revolvers and semiautomatics are similar, there are significant differences.

Revolvers

Revolvers derive their name from a part called the *cylinder* that revolves and holds the ammunition. The major assembly groups of a revolver are the *frame*, the *cylinder*, the *barrel* and the *grip*. (See Figure 1.)

The Frame

All important working components of a revolver are attached to the *frame*, which is composed of metal and can vary in size.

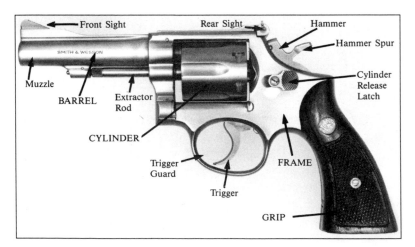

Figure 1.

2

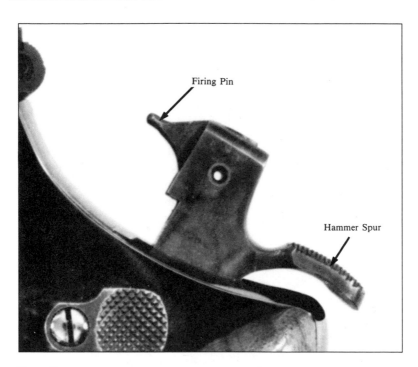

Firing Pin

Hammer Spur

Figure 2.

Attached to the frame, or housed in the frame, are several parts that assist your aiming and shooting, each of which has a special name and function.

The *hammer* (Figure 2), attached at the rear of the frame, falls from the cocked (ready-to-fire) position, causing the firing pin to strike the cartridge and the gun to fire. The rear portion of the hammer is called the *hammer spur,* which provides a gripping surface for your thumb so you can manually cock or uncock the gun. On some revolvers the hammers are concealed, not exposed; but exposed hammers are an advantage since they allow you to clearly determine when a handgun is cocked.

The *trigger* is located on the underside of the frame and, when pulled, causes the handgun to fire. The *trigger guard,* the metal frame protecting the trigger, is designed to reduce the possibility of accidental firing.

The *cylinder release* releases the cylinder for loading and unloading, allowing the cylinder to revolve freely for easy access.

Located on the top rear of the frame is a *rear sight*. Aligning it with the front sight, the shooter aims the revolver. Some revolvers have adjustable rear sights, permitting the shooter to adjust for more accurate aiming.

The Cylinder

The *cylinder* (Figure 3), which holds the cartridges ready for firing, contains *chambers* that normally hold five or six cartridges. Each time the hammer comes to the rear, the cylinder turns, bringing a fresh cartridge in line with the barrel and firing pin. Revolvers also may have an *extractor*, the operation and location of which can vary. All extractors are designed to remove cartridges from the cylinder.

Figure 3.

The Barrel

The metal tube through which the bullet passes on its way to the target is the *barrel*. The inside of a barrel is called the *bore* and is sized according to *caliber*. Calibers are measured and identified in hundredths of an inch (i.e., .22 caliber, .38 caliber) and in millimeters (i.e., 7.65mm caliber, 9mm caliber). The front end of the barrel where the bullet exits is the *muzzle.* The *front sight* is located above the muzzle on top of the barrel and should be aligned with the rear sight for aiming.

The Grip

The *grip* is the handgun's handle, designed to allow you to control the gun while you aim and shoot. Grips are usually composed of wood or molded plastic and are attached to the frame with screws.

Semiautomatics

Semiautomatic handguns (autoloaders) (Figure 4) differ from revolvers in basic operation. Semiautomatics are of various sizes, shapes and calibers, but they have one thing in common. When fired, they automatically extract and eject the empty case and chamber a new cartridge with each pull of the trigger. Cartridges are usually loaded in a magazine that is inserted into the grip of the gun (Figure 5).

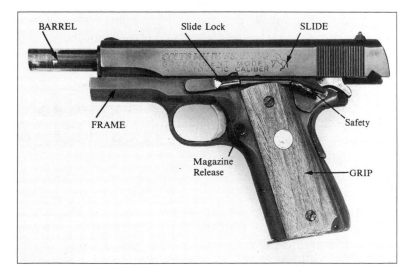

Figure 4.

5

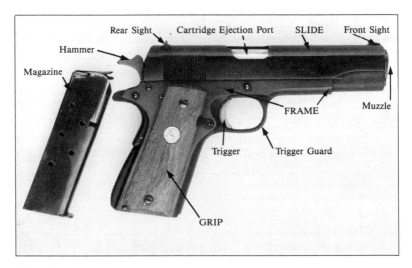

Figure 5.

Semiautomatics are composed of four major assembly groups: the *frame*, the *slide*, the *barrel* and the *grip*.

The Frame

The *frame* contains most of the moving parts that cause the semiautomatic to fire. The trigger and hammer are usually components of the frame and perform the same functions on semiautomatics as they do on revolvers. On hammerless semiautomatics, the firing pin is driven by an internal spring.

Another part usually located on the frame of semiautomatics is the *safety*, a back-up system to help prevent accidental firing. Since safeties are mechanical and can malfunction, preventing an accident is ultimately the responsibility of the individual handling the gun.

The Slide

The *slide* is located on top of the barrel and slides back and forth on the upper portion of the frame—thus its name. The slide contains the firing pin and the extractor. The slide's movement cocks the gun, chambers a cartridge for firing and ejects the spent cartridge.

The Barrel

The *barrel* on the semiautomatics has basically the same components as does a revolver's, with one major exception. Since a semiautomatic has no cylinder, the chamber for holding the cartridge during firing is at the rear of the barrel.

On some semiautomatics, the barrel is located inside the slide. Therefore, depending on the design of the handgun, the front and rear sights may be located either on the slide or on the barrel.

The Grip

As with the revolver, the *grip* of the semiautomatic is the portion you grasp. The grip of most semiautomatics contains the *magazine*, a metal container that holds the cartridges. The magazine can be removed from the grip for loading by activating the *magazine release*. The position of the release can vary with make and model; therefore, you should check the owner's manual for the specific location on your gun.

PART I
CHAPTER 1
WORKBOOK REVIEW

What are the two common types of handguns and the names of their assembly groups?

1. _Semi-autos_   2. _Revolvers_

grip

A. _Barrel_	A. _cylinder_
B. _Magazine_	B. _Barrel_
C. _hammer Slide_	C. _grip_
D. _frame_	D. _frame_

Briefly describe the function of the hammer.

move the firing pin to make it ~~firearm~~
hit cartridge.

The bore size is called the _caliber_ .

The end of the barrel where the bullet exits is the _muzzle_.

_____ .

Briefly describe the functions of the magazine and cylinder and how they differ.

magazine auto reloads -
holds many - easy to reload

cylinder - holds used
shells

NOTES

2. AMMUNITION

Because they are designed for different uses, handgun cartridges are available in a variety of types and sizes. To determine the best ammunition for your needs, you should understand their function, types and purposes.

Cartridges and Their Function

Modern metallic cartridges consist of four basic components: *case, priming compound* (referred to as primer), *propellant* (or powder) and *bullet.*

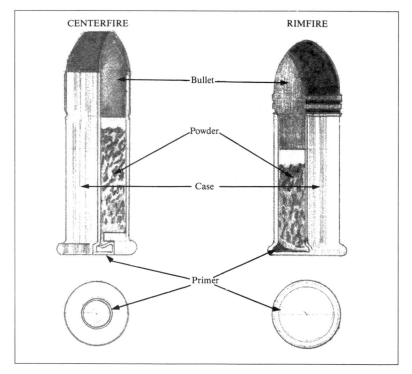

Figure 6.

While ammunition comes in many sizes, there are only two basic types — *centerfire* and *rimfire* — distinguished by the location of the primer. Most .22 caliber ammunition is rimfire, with

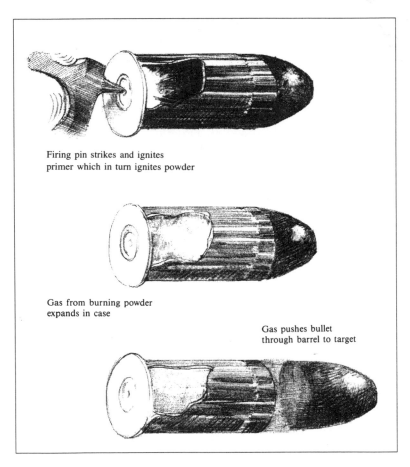

Firing pin strikes and ignites
primer which in turn ignites powder

Gas from burning powder
expands in case

Gas pushes bullet
through barrel to target

Figure 7.

the primer contained in the rim of the case. Larger caliber cartridges are centerfire, with the primer in the center of the case. (See Figure 6.)

When a cartridge is loaded in a chamber, the primer rests directly in front of the firing pin. When the trigger is pulled, the firing pin strikes and ignites the primer, providing flame that ignites the powder in the cartridge case. The burning powder rapidly generates a large volume of gas that creates the pressure that drives the bullet from the case and through the barrel to the target. (See Figure 7.)

Cartridge Designation and Identification

Although a cartridge appears to fit into the chamber or magazine, it may not be correct for that particular handgun. Firing the wrong ammunition can lead to a serious accident.

Make absolutely certain the ammunition you use is compatible with your handgun. There are several methods to assure that you have the right match of gun and ammunition. Center-fire cartridges are marked on the bottom of the case with caliber designation and manufacturer. Rimfire cartridges of .22 caliber are identified by the manufacturer's container or box. Likewise, handguns are marked on the slide or barrel, identifying the cartridge to be used (Figure 8). Make sure all the various designations are the same. In addition, check your owner's manual for guidelines.

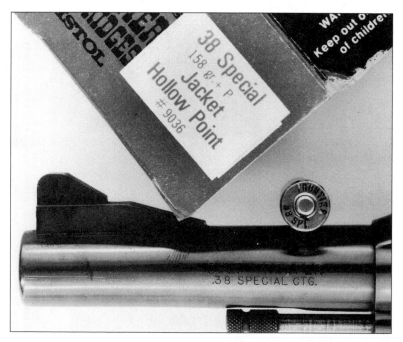

Figure 8. *Be sure you have the correct ammunition by checking the identification on the handgun, cartridge and cartridge box.*

Bullet Types

A range of ammunition calibers provide different bullet types from which to choose. Bullets may be designated as *soft-nosed*, *hollow-pointed* or *full-metal jacketed*. Soft-nosed and hollow-pointed bullets rapidly transfer energy to the target upon impact, while full-metal jacketed bullets are designed to pass through the target with relatively little loss of energy.

Figure 9. *From left to right are the soft-nosed lead bullet, a hollow point bullet and a full metal jacketed bullet.*

When using high velocity or magnum ammunition, you should keep in mind its greater penetration capabilities. This ammunition can penetrate walls and travel some distance before its energy has been expended. Some bullet types may fail to function in a semiautomatic; so, be sure the ammunition you select performs reliably.

The most common calibers used for protection are the .38 Special and the 9mm. These calibers can be purchased from sporting goods stores.

Care of Ammunition

Like your handgun, ammunition should be safely stored away from children and inexperienced or untrained adults. It should be kept dry and away from moisture and extreme heat. Fingerprints should be wiped from ammunition since acids, salts and perspiration may cause corrosion. Cartridges may also be penetrated and ruined by solvents and oils. Storing cartridges in leather cartridge belts may appear stylish, but the acids in leather can cause corrosion. Cartridges kept in your handgun should be replaced periodically with new ones. The older ammunition may be used in practice. When cared for properly, good quality, factory ammunition rarely misfires (fails to fire).

PART I
CHAPTER 2
WORKBOOK REVIEW

Cartridges are made up of what four components?

A. _Bullet_

B. _Primer_

C. _Case_

D. _Powder_

The two basic types of cartridges are _centerfire_

and _rim fire_ . Describe their distinguishing characteristics. _Primer's in middle on); around rim on._

Describe how you could determine whether your ammunition and gun are compatible. _Check gun, box, owner's man., & cartridge!_

The most common calibers used for protection are _9mm_

_____ and ~~XXXX~~ _.38_ .

Briefly describe some of the key points of proper ammunition care. _Keep clean. No oils, acids, fingerprints. Cool, dry, no intense heat. New. don't keep in leather._

15

NOTES

3. HANDGUN OPERATION

Loading, preparing to fire and unloading are general operations of common handguns, whether they be single action revolvers, double action revolvers or semiautomatics. Handgun operation may vary according to manufacturer and model; therefore, only basic guidelines will be covered in this chapter. Follow-up with a thorough review of the owner's manual for your gun. Since procedures in this handbook are presented from the right-hand perspective, left-handers may need to adapt the following information.

REVOLVERS

There are literally thousands of revolver designs, but almost all modern revolvers belong in one of two categories: *single action* and *double action*. *Single action* means the trigger performs a single function—to release the hammer. The hammer must be hand-cocked before the gun can be fired. *Double action* means the trigger has two functions—to cock the hammer, then to release it. A double action revolver can be cocked and fired simply by pulling the trigger.

Single Action Revolver

Pulling the hammer of a single action revolver to the rear, you will hear and feel three clicks. The first click position keeps the firing pin off a live cartridge when the gun is loaded. The second click (half cock position) releases the cylinder to move freely for loading and unloading. The third click (full cock position) cocks the revolver for firing.

To Load:

1. With finger off trigger, hold revolver in left hand with muzzle pointed downward.
2. With right thumb, pull hammer to the second click (half cock position) allowing cylinder to turn freely.
3. With right thumb, open loading gate (Figure 10).
4. Align empty chamber with loading opening (loading port) by turning the cylinder (Figure 11).

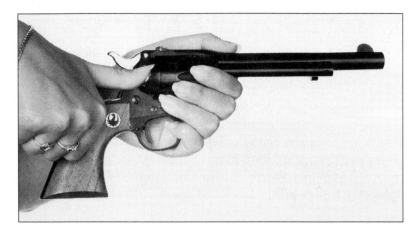

Figure 10.

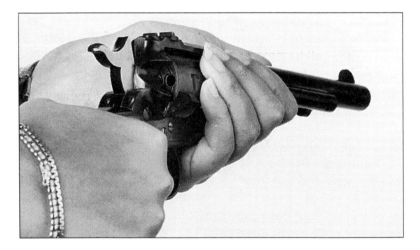

Figure 11.

5. With right hand, insert cartridge and rotate cylinder to next chamber. Repeat process until desired amount of ammunition has been inserted. (See Figure 12.)
6. Close loading gate.

NOTE: Whether the gun is unloaded, partially loaded or fully loaded, *always* follow all the gun safety rules.

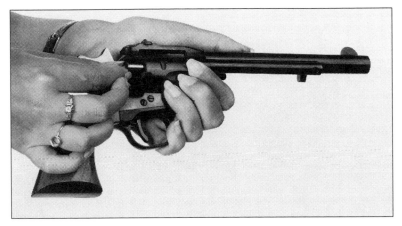

Figure 12

To Cock:
1. With finger off trigger and with left thumb on hammer spur, pull hammer to the third click (full cock position) (Figure 13).

Figure 13.

To Uncock:
1. With finger off trigger, place right thumb firmly on cocked hammer.

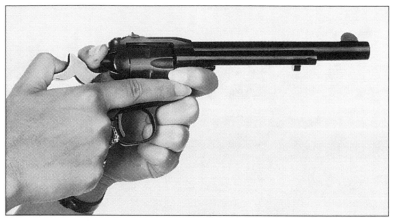

Figure 14.

2. Place left thumb between frame and hammer (Figure 14).
3. Pull trigger to release hammer and lower it gently against the thumb (Figure 15).

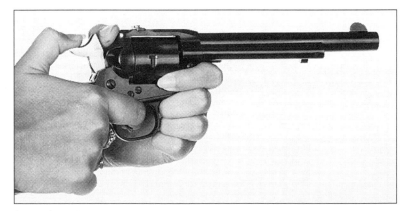

Figure 15.

4. Continuing to pull trigger, and maintaining control of hammer with right thumb, carefully remove left thumb, slowly lowering hammer all the way down.
5. Remove finger from trigger and, with left thumb, return hammer to first click (safety) position.

To Unload:
1. With finger off trigger, hold revolver in left hand with muzzle pointed downward.
2. With right thumb, pull hammer to half cock position, allowing cylinder to turn freely.
3. With right thumb, open loading gate.
4. Align loaded chamber with port (opening) (Figure 16).

Figure 16.

5. Elevate muzzle, rotate cylinder with right hand, allowing cartridges to fall out of chambers. NOTE: Ejector rod can be used to assist removal of cartridges or empty cases, if necessary. (See Figure 17.)
6. Rotate cylinder, visually checking to ensure all cartridges have been removed.
7. Close loading gate and pull trigger, lowering hammer to down position.

Double Action Revolver
Double action revolvers are considered the most modern revolvers and are by far the most commonly used for personal

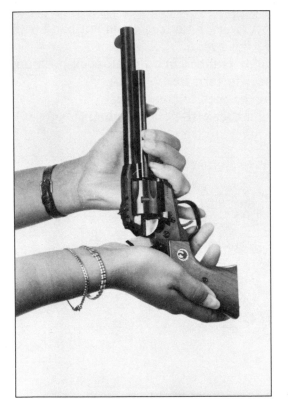

Figure 17.

protection because they are so easy to operate. They can be cocked and fired simply by pulling the trigger. In addition, they are easy to load and unload.

1. With finger off trigger, hold revolver with right hand.
2. Operate cylinder release with right thumb (Figure 18).
3. With revolver pointed downward, push cylinder open with the two middle fingers of left hand (Figure 19).
4. Holding revolver with left hand, point muzzle downward, load cartridges in cylinder chamber with right hand (Figure 20).

Figure 18.

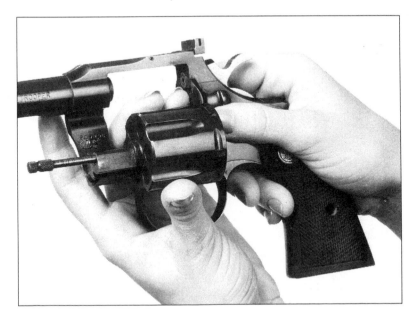

Figure 19.

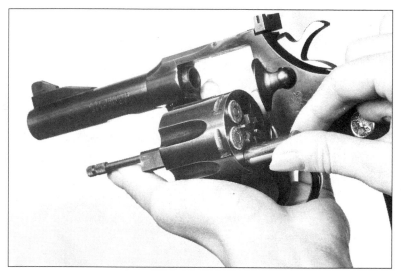

Figure 20.

5. Regrip revolver with right hand, push cylinder closed with left thumb.

NOTE: (1) Left-handed shooters should also use this loading process.

(2) Whether the gun is unloaded, partially loaded or fully loaded, *always* follow all the gun safety rules.

To Cock:

1. With finger off trigger, cock hammer with thumb of free hand by pulling it all the way to the rear until it stops.

To Uncock:

1. With finger off trigger, place right thumb firmly on cocked hammer.
2. Place left thumb between frame and hammer (Figure 21).
3. Controlling the hammer with the right thumb, pull trigger to release hammer and gently lower hammer against left thumb (Figure 22).

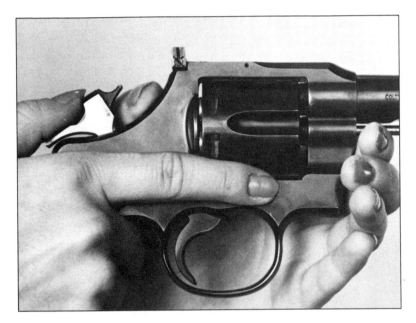

Figure 21.

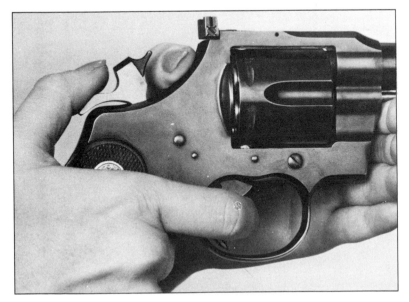

Figure 22.

4. Remove finger from trigger (Figures 23a).
5. Continuing to control the hammer with the right thumb, remove the left thumb and carefully lower hammer (Figure 23b).

To Unload:

1. With finger off trigger, hold revolver in right hand.
2. Operate cylinder release with right thumb.
3. With revolver pointed downward, push cylinder open with two middle fingers of left hand (Figure 24).
4. Place left thumb on ejector rod.
5. Elevate muzzle and firmly push ejector rod completely to rear, catching cartridges in right hand. Inspect each cylinder to ensure all cartridges have been removed. (See Figure 25.)

Figure 23a.

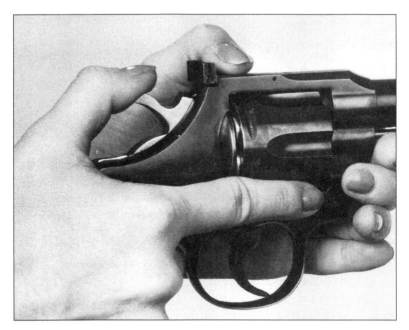

Figure 23b.

Figure 24.

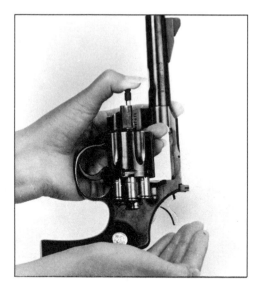

Figure 25.

Semiautomatics

The identifying characteristic of a semiautomatic pistol is that it automatically and instantly reloads and recocks itself with each pull of the trigger after the first shot is fired and will continue to do so until the magazine is empty. This type of operation is termed *semiautomatic* because only one round is fired for each pull of the trigger. (Firearms that continue to fire when the trigger is held are known as *full automatics*.)

Semiautomatics may be of either *hammerless* or *visible hammer* configuration. Hammerless models, as the name implies, have no visible hammer and employ an internal firing pin mechanism. Hammerless semiautomatics are cocked simply by pulling the slide fully to the rear and releasing it. This action also loads a cartridge into the chamber.

Semiautomatics with visible hammers may have either *single action* or *double action* firing mechanisms. With single action models, the hammer must be moved to the full cock position before the first shot is fired. This is accomplished by manually pulling the hammer to the cocked position or by withdrawing and releasing the slide. Double action semiautomatics can be

28

fired simply by pulling the trigger. With most double action semiautomatics, one also has the option of manually cocking the hammer for the first shot.

Because of many differences in semiautomatics, the loading, cocking and unloading procedures vary greatly. Be sure to refer to the owner's manual or consult a competent gunsmith if you are unsure of the proper procedures to follow when performing these operations.

To Load:

1. With finger off trigger, hold pistol in right hand.
2. Activate the magazine release and remove magazine. NOTE: Location of the magazine release will vary. Check owner's manual. (See Figure 26.)

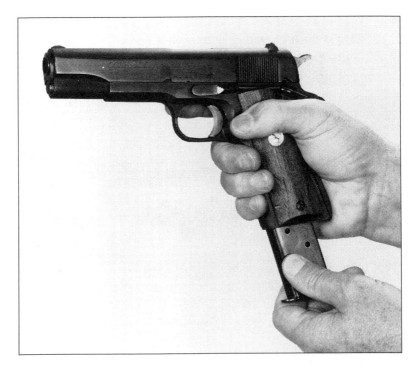

Figure 26.

3. Place thumb and forefinger of free hand on rear portion of slide, move slide to rear and lock open with slide stop, if gun is so equipped (Figure 27).
4. Look into chamber to ensure it is not loaded (Figure 28).
5. Load magazine. With magazine in either hand and rounded portion facing away from you, push cartridges down and to rear. Repeat process until loaded. (See Figure 29.)
6. With finger off trigger, return pistol to right hand.
7. Insert loaded magazines into handgun grip (Figure 30).
8. With finger off trigger, grasp rear portion of the slide with free hand, move to rear and release, loading a cartridge into the chamber. *The gun is now cocked and ready to fire.* (See Figure 31.)

NOTE: If you wish to place a loaded magazine in the gun but not load the chamber, begin at number *6* and substitute the following procedure:

7. Grasp rear portion of slide with free hand, move to rear and release.
8. With safety off, pull trigger to uncock the gun.

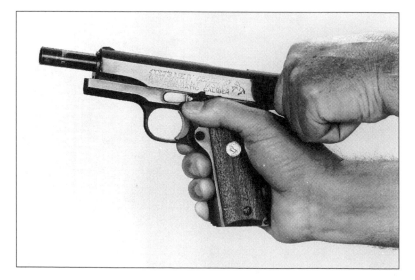

Figure 27.

Figure 28.

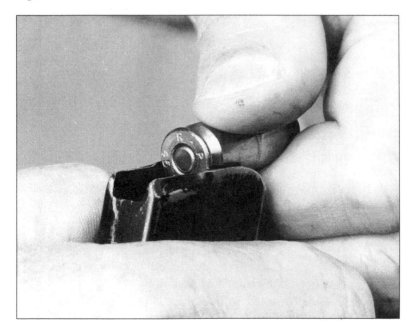

Figure 29.

Figure 30.

9. Insert loaded magazine into magazine well.
NOTE: Whether the gun is unloaded, partially loaded or fully loaded, *always* follow all the gun safety rules.

To Uncock:

As previously noted, semiautomatics vary in operation. Some designs allow uncocking of a loaded semiautomatic; some don't. Such differences make it impossible to cover procedures for uncocking semiautomatics herein. You should check the manu-

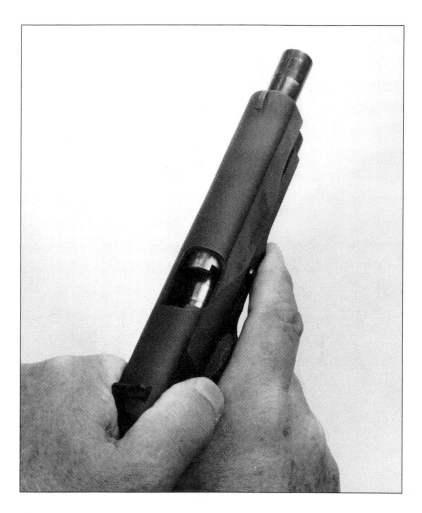

Figure 31.

facturer's manual for your gun or consult an instructor or a competent gunsmith.

To Unload:

1. With finger off trigger, hold handgun in right hand.
2. Release magazine and remove from gun.

3. Place thumb and forefinger of free hand on rear portion of slide and pull slide to rear, ejecting cartridge from chamber. And, as always, check chamber to be sure it is unloaded. (See Figure 32.)

NOTE: When storing an unloaded semiautomatic, close the action and uncock it to release tension on springs.

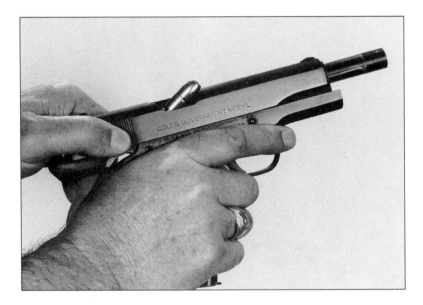

Figure 32.

PART I
CHAPTER 3
WORKBOOK REVIEW

What type of revolver can be cocked and fired simply by pulling the trigger?

double-action revolver

What type of revolver is most frequently used for personal protection and why?

Same. They're easy to use & easy to load&unload.

The loading, cocking and unloading processes differ greatly on which type of handgun?

Semis. They're all very different

Briefly outline the steps for the loading, cocking, uncocking and unloading for the handgun(s) you will use.

NOTES

4. SAFETY

Competitive target shooters have made their sport one of the safest in the world because they recognize the basic responsibility of *all* gunowners and shooters: SAFETY. Becoming a safe shooter is no different from becoming a safe driver. You start with a good working *knowledge* of the equipment, learn the basic *skills* of handling it correctly, and develop a *positive attitude* toward always using your knowledge and skills in a responsible manner. A positive attitude toward firearm safety is essential. Without it, an individual sooner or later will get into trouble.

Think SAFETY every time you pick up a gun. One of the most important skills you will ever learn is handling and shooting a handgun safely.

Learning is reinforced by practice. Regular practice of correct procedures with your handgun helps you develop good safety habits.

NRA Gun Safety Rules

The first focus is simply handling a gun safely. Usually, your handgun will be in your home or business, not on the shooting range. In fact, you'll find most of your time is spent just handling a firearm, rather than shooting it.

Three key rules apply under *all* circumstances when handling a gun. If you can't remember anything else, remember the first one, the "Golden Rule of Gun Safety".

The Fundamental NRA Rules for Safe Gun Handling Are:

- **Always keep the gun pointed in a safe direction.** Whether you are shooting or simply handling your gun, never point the muzzle at yourself or at others. Common sense should dictate which direction is safest, depending on your location and other conditions. Generally, it is safest to point the gun upward or downward. (See Figure 33.)

- **Always keep your finger off the trigger until ready to shoot.** There's a natural tendency to place your finger on the trigger when holding a gun. Avoid it! Your finger can

Figure 33.

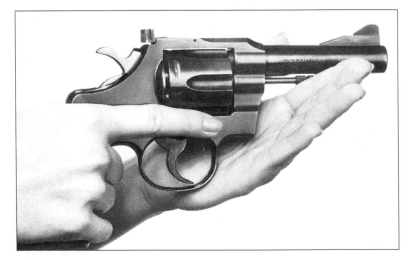

Figure 34.

rest on the trigger guard or better yet around the grip of the gun. Trigger guards are to prevent the trigger from getting accidently bumped. (See Figure 34.)

- **Always keep the gun unloaded until ready to use.** Whenever you pick up any gun, immediately open the action and check (visually if possible) to see that the chamber is unloaded. If the gun has a magazine, remove it and make sure it's empty. If you do not know how to open the gun's action, leave it alone and get help from someone who does. (See Figure 35.)

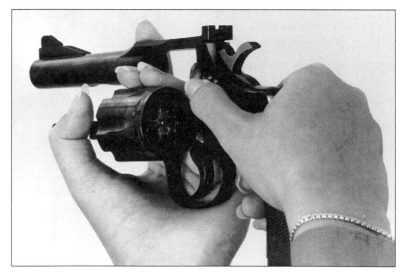

Figure 35.

All safety rules are important, but the first rule is the foundation of gun safety. If you always keep the muzzle pointed in a safe direction, you will virtually eliminate the likelihood of accidentally injuring yourself or others. However, bullets can penetrate walls, floors and ceilings and travel considerable distances.

The remaining rules decrease the chance of an accident's occurring. Read them, know them, understand them, but, most importantly, *follow them!*

When Using or Storing a Gun Aways Follow These NRA Rules:

- **Be sure the gun is safe to operate.** Just like other tools, guns need regular maintenance to remain operable. Regular cleaning and proper storage are part of the gun's general upkeep. If there is any question concerning a gun's ability to function, a competent gunsmith should look at it.

- **Know how to safely use the gun.** Before handling a gun, learn how it operates. Know its basic parts, how to open and close the action safely and how to remove safely any ammunition from the gun or magazine. Remember, a gun's mechanical safety device is never foolproof. Nothing can ever replace safe gun handling.

- **Use only the correct ammunition for your gun.** Only BBs, pellets, cartridges or shells designed for a particular gun can be fired safely in that gun. Most guns have the ammunition type stamped on the barrel. Ammunition can be identified by information printed on the box and sometimes stamped on the cartridge. Do not shoot the gun if there is any question about the compatibility of the gun and ammunition.

- **Know your target and what is beyond.** Be absolutely sure you have identified your target beyond any doubt. Equally important, be aware of the area beyond your target. This means observing your prospective area of fire before you shoot. Never fire in a direction in which there are people or any other potential for mishap. Think first. Shoot second.

- **Wear eye and ear protection as appropriate.** Guns are loud and the noise can cause hearing damage. They can also emit debris and hot gas that could cause eye injury. For these reasons, safety glasses and ear protectors are strongly recommended. (See Figure 36.)

- **Never use alcohol or drugs before or while shooting.** Alcohol, as well as any other substance likely to impair normal mental or physical functions must not be used before or while handling or shooting guns.

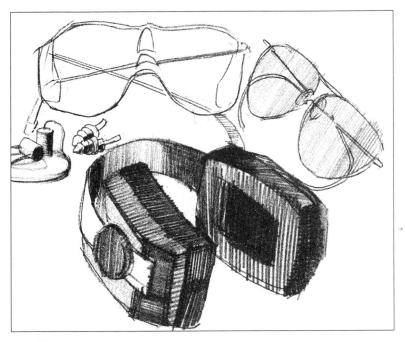

Figure 36.

- **Store guns so that they are not accessible to unauthorized persons.** Several factors should be considered when you decide where and how you intend to store your guns. Your particular needs will be a major part of the consideration. Safe and secure storage requires that untrained individuals (especially children) be denied access to your guns.

Be aware that certain types of guns and many shooting situations require additional safety precautions.

These shooting safety rules cannot be stressed too strongly. *You* are responsible for knowing and following these rules every time you handle or shoot a gun. The rules must be applied to every type of gun in every situation. Safety with guns is a matter of knowing safety rules and of having the self-discipline to observe and to apply them — always.

PART I
CHAPTER 4
WORKBOOK REVIEW

What are the three essential elements that a person must have to handle a handgun safely?

1. _Always keep gun pointed in safe dir._
2. _"   "   " finger off trigger 'til ready to shoot._
3. _"   "   " gun unloaded until ready to use._

Of these, which one will determine whether you're always going

to be safe? _ y all. #3, esp._ .

What is the "Golden Rule of Gun Safety" and why do you think it has been so designated?

1. _If you're not pointing it at anyone, no one can get hurt._

Switch

What three rules apply under all circumstances when handling a gun?
1. _Knowledge_
2. _Skills_
3. _positive attitude_

If you are handling a gun, who is the person always responsible for pointing it in a safe direction?

you.

NOTES

5. SELECTING A HANDGUN

Considerable work in evaluating and selecting a proper handgun for personal protection has already been done for you. The majority of law enforcement officers who use a handgun for the same purpose choose a .38 caliber double action revolver with an exposed hammer and a four-inch barrel. The experience of major police departments indicates that this type of handgun is the simplest and safest to use — and the most reliable. Semiautomatics tend to be more complicated to operate and are prone to jam.

Whatever your choice, be sure to do your homework before you make a final selection. Visit a local gun shop and shooting range; ask a lot of questions. Manufacturers' catalogues and your local library are also good sources of information. The following two chapters of this handbook provide basic information regarding the most commonly used handguns and their operation.

In selecting the right handgun, you should:

1. Seek advice from a handgun expert and purchase your gun from a reputable dealer.

Figure 37.

2. Determine if your handgun use will be multi-purpose or specific. Then, consider the best caliber weight and barrel length for such use.
3. Decide how much you want to spend. Remember, you usually get what you pay for!
4. Study the various makes and models available.
5. Consider the simplicity of operation and cleaning.
6. Be sure the handgun fits your hand.
7. Check availability and cost of ammunition, based on the amount of shooting you plan to do.
8. Know the manufacturers. Are parts and service available and are they likely to be in the future? Buying quality brand names will generally ensure quick repair, if necessary.
9. Read the warranty or guarantee.
10. Determine if the particular handgun has a record of trouble-free dependability.

PART I
CHAPTER 5
WORKBOOK REVIEW

Based on the law enforcement's experience, describe the characteristics of a good handgun for personal protection.

Where might you find information concerning the types of handguns?

NOTES

6. CLEANING AND STORAGE

With proper care, cleaning and storage, your handgun should function reliably for many years. Preventive maintenance will keep your handgun in good working condition.

Inspect your handgun periodically to be sure that it is in good working condition and that it functions smoothly. If you find any irregularities, have a competent gunsmith inspect your handgun and repair it, if necessary.

Cleaning the Handgun

Gun cleaning kits may be purchased from gun stores and at some department stores. To clean your handgun, you will need a cleaning rod, bore brush and patches, cleaning solvent, oil, small brush (old toothbrush) and a soft cloth. Since cleaning rods and bore brushes are sized according to caliber, be sure to choose the appropriate caliber for your gun.

A new handgun or one brought out of prolonged storage should be thoroughly cleaned before shooting. Accumulated moisture, dirt or grease can interfere with efficient and safe operation.

Handguns should be cleaned after firing. Always unload your gun and remove any ammunition from the cleaning area

Figure 38. Having the right materials and equipment to clean your handgun is important. Be sure that the barrel brush is the right size for the caliber of your gun.

before beginning the process. The gun's action should remain open during cleaning.

1. Place bore brush on cleaning rod, wet it with cleaning solvent and work it back and forth in the bore to loosen residue and fouling. Repeat as necessary. (See Figures 39a and 39b.)
2. To remove the loosened residue and fouling from the bore, run a series of patches through it (using the rod with jag to secure patch) until they emerge clean. Finally, push an oiled patch through the bore. (See Figures 40a and 40b.)

NOTE: With revolvers, clean cylinder chambers in the same manner.

3. Clean any remaining foreign material from the gun with a small brush or cloth (Figure 41a).
4. With a lightly oiled cloth, wipe all exposed metal surfaces (Figure 41b).

After the handgun has been cleaned for storage, avoid touching the metal parts with your hand. Perspiration and skin oils can cause rusting.

Storage of Handguns

The rule for firearms storage dictates that no firearm should be accessible to children and/or careless or unauthorized adults. The standard of care should be reasonable and based on the fundamental responsibility of every gunowner. Some circumstances may require minimal precautions, as in the case of a policeman living alone, or additional precautions may be unique to a particular situation, such as a house filled with children. Any firearm must be stored with safety in mind. A firearm not likely to be used for defensive purposes must be stored in such a manner that it will not be readily accessible to children or careless and unauthorized adults. Ammunition should be stored in a like manner.

When a firearm is kept accessible for personal protection, safety must be foremost. A defensive firearm should be kept out of view and every precaution should be taken to prevent careless or unauthorized use. (See Figure 42.)

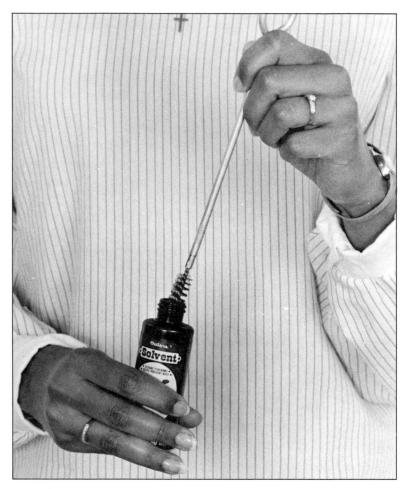

Figure 39a.

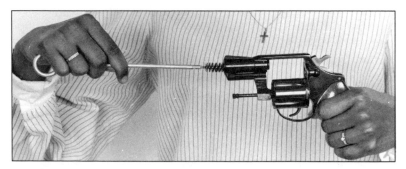

Figure 39b.

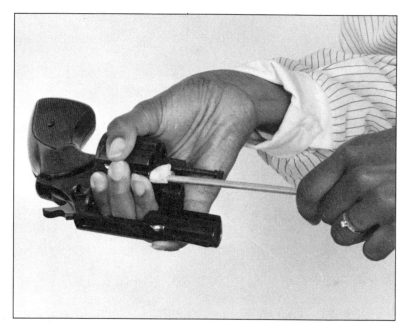

Figure 40a.

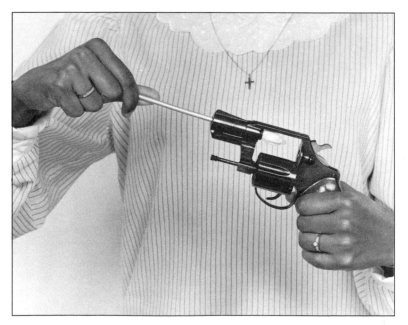

Figure 40b.

Figure 41a.

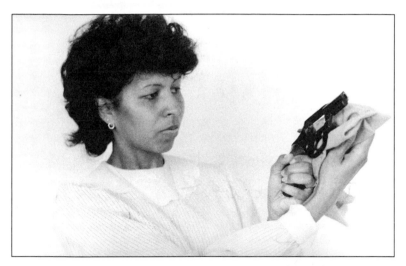

Figure 41b.

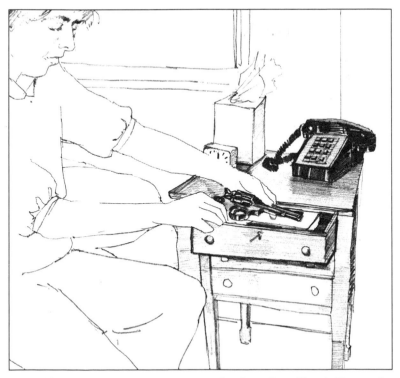

Figure 42. *Think about where to store your handgun. You will probably want it accessible to you, but not to others.*

PART I
CHAPTER 6
WORKBOOK REVIEW

What items will you need to clean a handgun?

natural solvent
oil
cleanpatches
brush

What is the key safety rule for cleaning your handgun?

do it a lot.

The rule for storing a firearm is _____

_____ .

The standard of care that should be employed in the storage

of a firearm is _____ .

NOTES

PART TWO:

BASIC SHOOTING SKILLS

1. LEARNING THE FUNDAMENTALS

As a new handgun owner, you may ask, "Why do I need to shoot at paper targets if I intend to use a gun only for protection?" Law enforcement officers have learned that practicing on targets helps develop the confidence and good habits required to shoot well under adverse conditions. Under stress, a person will shoot as he or she has been trained to shoot. Therefore, range practice needs to be based on learning and practicing the *fundamentals of handgun shooting.*

A definition of "fundamentals" may be useful here. Fundamentals are the minimum "essential" components of a function or structure, in this case those related to shooting a handgun. You will need to know and to practice the following fundamentals to accomplish your goal of becoming an effective shooter:

1. Shooting Position
2. Shot Preparation
3. Sight Alignment Control
4. Trigger Control
5. Follow-Through

***

1. Shooting Position

Shooting position is simply: (a) the position of your body; and (b) the position of the handgun during the act of shooting. *Position of the body* is the alignment of the body parts in the act of shooting and their relationship to the target. Positioning the body is the first step toward assuming all shooting positions. Two conditions are essential for a good position: first, you must be comfortable and relaxed, attaining as natural a body position as possible without straining muscles; second, your position must be aligned with the target. The *position of*

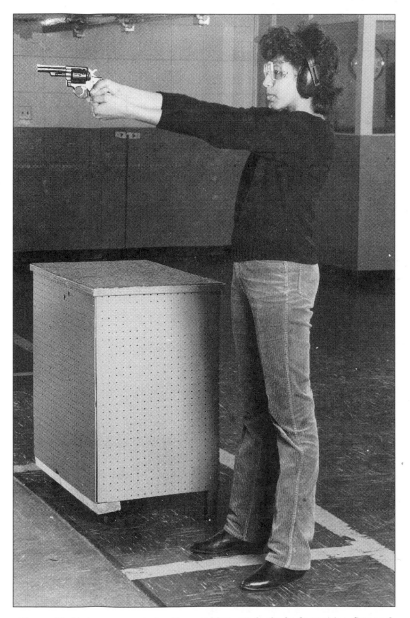

Figure 43. *To learn a good shooting position, study the body position first and then the position of the handgun.*

the handgun is the proper positioning of the handgun in relation to the body and the target.

A good shooting position provides the shooter with a solid, steady hold on the target. A variety of positions can be assumed when shooting a handgun, but we will concentrate on three basic ones: *benchrest, two-handed standing* and *one-handed standing*.

2. Shot Preparation

During the shot preparation, the shooter will concentrate on two important functions: aiming and breath control.

Aiming is the process of lining up your gun with the target, involving the relationship between four objects — the eye, the rear sight, the front sight and the target. Proper sight alignment, the key to aiming, is critical to successful handgun shooting. *Sight alignment* involves the relationship between your eye and the rear and front sights of the gun. Achieving and maintaining this alignment are essential if a shot is to hit the desired area on a target.

When the sights are correctly aligned, the front sight is centered in the rear sight notch and the top of the front sight is even with the top of the rear sight. Once the sights are aligned with each other, the aligned sights are then put into the center of the target. (See Figure 44.)

Because every breath causes the body to move slightly, you must control your breathing when you shoot. *Breath Control* minimizes unnecessary body movements. Holding your breath too long can also cause increased movement; therefore, you should learn to fire your shot within 6 to 8 seconds of your breath control procedure.

You are now ready to proceed to the next two fundamentals, the most important to firing a successful shot: sight alignment control and trigger control. These procedures are performed simultaneously.

3. Sight Alignment Control

Sight alignment control is the process of maintaining proper sight alignment until the shot is completed. The critical point

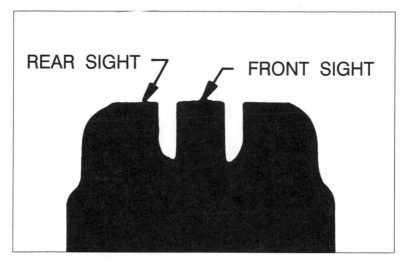

REAR SIGHT ⌐   ⌐ FRONT SIGHT

Figure 44.

to remember is that sight alignment must be sustained during the process of a controlled trigger pull. Regular practice will help you learn to control sight alignment.

4. Trigger Control

The importance of proper trigger control cannot be over-stated. The other fundamentals are of little use unless you learn to pull the trigger straight back without disturbing sight alignment. This may require some trial-and-error testing on your part. Once you achieve a smooth pull, remember the technique and practice it.

5. Follow-Through

With most physical skills, you perform an action in which follow-through is essential to completion. In bowling, your arm must continue its forward swing after the ball is released. Likewise, the final step in handgun shooting is the follow-through; immediately following the shot, you must maintain your shooting position for the proper follow-through. Because it is impossible to determine precisely when the bullet leaves the barrel, failure to maintain position – or follow-through – can affect the path of the bullet.

PART II
CHAPTER 1
WORKBOOK REVIEW

Briefly define fundamentals.

List the fundamentals of handgun shooting.

1. _____

2. _____

3. _____

4. _____

5. _____

What are the two conditions essential for a good shooting position?

Aiming involves the relationship of what four objects?

1. _____

2. _____

3. _____

4. _____

Describe the proper sight alignment.

Explain why sight alignment control and trigger control are so critical to hitting the target.

What elements make for good trigger control?

NOTES

2. FIRING YOUR FIRST SHOTS

Now that you are familiar with each of the fundamentals, you are ready to take the steps that will help you achieve positive results as you apply them—in practice. All handgun owners should spend time on a range, becoming familiar with the operation of their firearms. Locate a range in your area for this purpose. Each time you go to practice, carefully review the fundamentals and safety rules.

An excellent first target is a large grocery bag or the blank side of a paper target placed about 10 to 20 feet in front of the firing line and on the same level as the bench. A bullseye type target is not necessary at this point.

Figure 45. *Using a blank target will help you to concentrate on proper sight alignment—the key to successful pistol shooting.*

THE BENCHREST POSITION

The fundamentals of shooting your handgun can best be applied first from a benchrest position. This position offers a steady support, allowing you to direct your concentration toward sight alignment and trigger control. A sandbag or some other support may be used to position hands and gun at a suitable level.

When learning any shooting position, you should follow four basic steps. Apply them in learning the benchrest position:

Step 1. Study the Position — learn what a good benchrest (or other) position looks like by studying the picture(s) in this handbook.

Step 2. Practice the Position Without Handgun — learn to put your feet, legs, body and arms in the correct position as you sit or kneel behind the bench (or stand behind the firing line). Practice until the position becomes comfortable and familiar.

Step 3. Practice the Position With Handgun — next add the unloaded handgun to the position you have already assumed. After achieving a proper grip, adjust position until you are comfortable and familiar with it.

Step 4. Align Position With Target — align your position so the handgun points naturally at the target. (From the benchrest position you can make vertical adjustments on the target by adjusting the height of the sandbag/support. Horizontal adjustments should be made by moving the body left or right.) Primary characteristics of the Benchrest Position are:

- **Position of Body** (See Figure 46)
  1. Shooter sits or kneels behind the table or bench facing the target.
  2. Both arms are fully extended directly in front of the face.
  3. Wrists rest on support.

- **Position of Handgun** (See Figure 47)
  1. Handgun is held with both hands in alignment with the shooting eye.

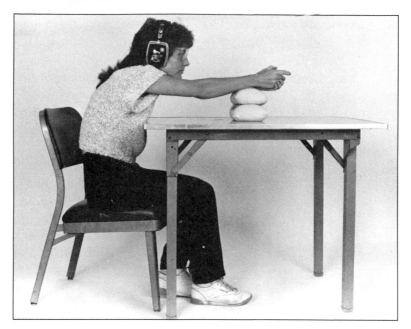

Figure 46.

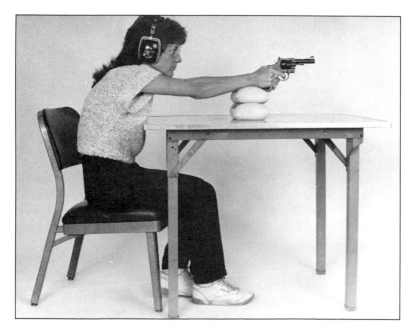

Figure 47.

- ## Assuming the Position
  1. Sit or kneel behind the table facing the target.
  2. Attain a proper grip:
     a. Keeping finger off trigger, hold the handgun in the nonshooting hand; then place the handgun between the thumb and forefinger of the shooting hand. (See Figure 48a.)
     b. While pushing the handgun firmly to the rear of the shooting hand, wrap the lower three fingers of the shooting hand around the grip (Figure 48b).
     c. Place the heel of the nonshooting hand against the heel of the shooting hand, with thumb resting on top of the shooting hand thumb. (See Figure 49a.)
     d. Wrap the fingers of the nonshooting hand firmly around the fingers of the shooting hand. (See Figure 49b.)
  3. With both arms fully extended directly in front of the face, position the gun on the support (if necessary, support can also be placed under the elbows). (See Figure 50.)
  4. Position gun sights in alignment with your shooting eye, pivoting the pistol on the sandbag as needed.

- ## Dry Firing
Once you are in position at the bench, dry firing (shooting without ammunition) will help you practice the fundamentals of firing a shot. In addition to being a great way to practice sight alignment and trigger control, dry firing is done with no ammunition; thus, no expense.

Dry firing gives you an opportunity to practice handling and operating a handgun. At the end of a dry-firing session, you should be familiar with cocking your handgun and you will have a "feel" for the amount of pressure necessary to pull the trigger. When dry firing with a semiautomatic pistol, do so with the empty magazine in the grip.

Practice dry firing frequently, but always make absolutely certain the handgun is unloaded. All safety rules apply in dry firing, just as they do when the gun is loaded.

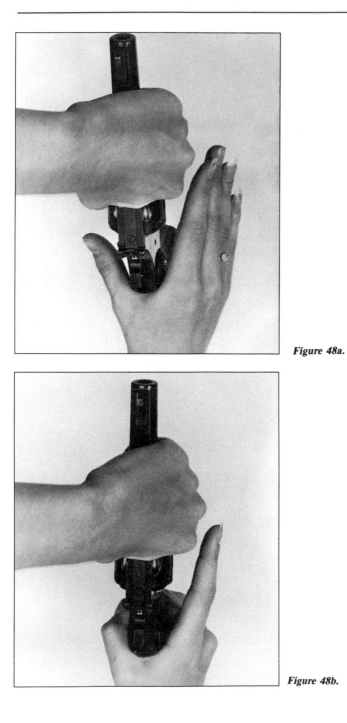

Figure 48a.

Figure 48b.

Figure 49a.

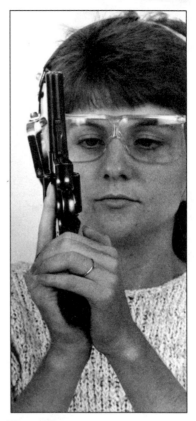

Figure 49b.

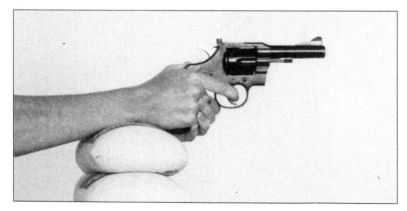

Figure 50.

• Live Firing

After you have dry fired and feel confident in your ability to perform the five fundamentals successfully, you are ready to fire your first shot. Be sure to review and apply all safety rules, and remember to use ear and eye protection. To prepare for your live-fire shooting exercises, take your position at the bench with your ammunition and handgun. You are now ready for the following exercises:

1. Single-shot Exercise

In this exercise, you will load and fire one cartridge at a time at the center of a blank target. Take your time and apply all of the handgun shooting fundamentals. Load, fire and unload your handgun five times or more in this exercise. (See Figure 52.)

2. Five-shot Group Exercise

Place a blank target down range and again take your position at the bench. For this exercise, load five cartridges into your handgun. If using a revolver, manually cock it for each shot. A semiautomatic does not require manual cocking after the first shot. After you have fired these five rounds of ammunition, you will notice that they form a group on the target. This exercise should be repeated several times.

3. Sight Adjustment

Most new shooters are happy if their first shots hit the target. With practice, your shots should begin hitting in the same area, forming smaller and smaller groups. Do not worry if these groups are not in the center of the target. On many handguns, you can affect the placement of the *shot group* by adjusting the rear sight. The rule of adjustment is to move the rear sight in the same direction you want the group to move. If your five-shot group is low and to the left of center, move your rear sights up and to the right. To adjust the sight on some handguns, you will need a small screwdriver. Before making adjustments, be sure the gun is unloaded. (Some

Figure 51. *Dry firing and live firing under the supervision of NRA Certified Instructors is the best way to learn the fundamentals.*

handguns have fixed sights that can only be adjusted by a competent gunsmith.)

After you have moved the rear sight, fire three shots. If they form a group in the center of your target, continue to the next exercise. If your shot group is still off center, continue moving the rear sight (with gun unloaded) and firing small groups until they are centered.

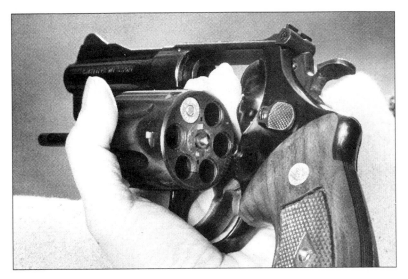

Figure 52. *The single shot exercise not only teaches you how to shoot, but just as important, how to safely load and unload your handgun.*

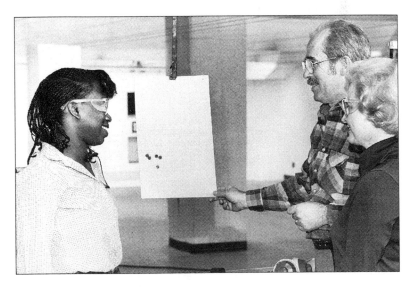

Figure 53. *Once you place five shots in a group on your target, you may need to adjust your sights so the group will be in the center of the target. This is done by moving the sights in the direction that you wish to move the shots on your target.*

4. Double Action Firing Exercise

If you have a double action revolver, you should now practice double action shooting. The purpose of this exercise is to learn how to cock and fire the gun by pulling the trigger. Load five cartridges and practice double action firing. Repeat this exercise as necessary.

***

These exercises provide a basic initiation to handgun shooting. However, if you are to maintain or improve your skill, you must practice regularly.

PART II
CHAPTER 2
WORKBOOK REVIEW

What is the advantage of practice-shooting from the benchrest position?

What are the four steps in learning any shooting position?

1. _____
2. _____
3. _____
4. _____

What is dry firing and what are its advantages?

What is a shot group?

How would you determine when your sights need adjusting?

The rule for sight adjustment is _____

_____ .

NOTES

3. OTHER HANDGUN SHOOTING POSITIONS

Once you have become familiar with the fundamentals from the benchrest position, you may apply them to other common positions for handgun shooting: the two-handed standing position (and point-shoulder variation) and the one-handed standing position. As you learn and practice these positions, again be sure to follow the safety rules and always keep the muzzle pointed in a safe direction.

Apply the four basic steps you followed in learning the benchrest position:

1. Study the position.
2. Practice the position without handgun.
3. Practice the position with handgun.
4. Align position with target. For the following positions make vertical adjustments to align with the target by moving arms up or down. Horizontal adjustments should be made by adjusting foot position.

TWO-HANDED STANDING POSITION

One of the quickest and most natural positions to assume is the two-handed standing position, the primary characteristics of which are:

* **Position of Body** (See Figure 54)
   1. Feet shoulder-width apart with body weight distributed equally on both feet.
   2. Arms fully extended in front of face.

* **Position of Handgun** (See Figure 55)
   1. Handgun is held with both hands in alignment with the shooting eye.

* **Assuming the Two-Handed Standing Position**
   1. Move to the firing point.
   2. Face the target.
   3. Attain the proper grip:
      a. Keeping finger off trigger, hold the handgun in the nonshooting hand, then place handgun between

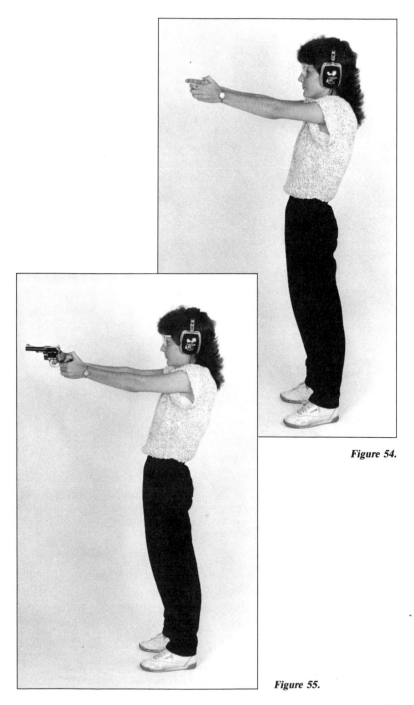

Figure 54.

Figure 55.

Figure 56. *There are two ways of holding a handgun with two hands. The top photograph shows the wrap around method where one hand is wrapped around the other. The bottom photograph shows the cup and saucer method where the gripping hand is placed in the palm of the other hand.*

the thumb and forefinger of the shooting hand.

b. Pushing the handgun to the rear of the shooting hand, wrap the lower three fingers firmly around the grip.

c. Place heel of the nonshooting hand against heel of the shooting hand with thumb resting on top of the shooting hand thumb.

d. Wrap fingers of the nonshooting hand firmly around the fingers of the shooting hand.

4. Extend arms toward target.

5. Position sights in alignment with shooting eye.

POINT-SHOULDER VARIATION

Point-shoulder, a variation of the two-handed standing position, allows the shooter to simply *point* the handgun at the target. Instead of aiming the handgun, a shooter places the handgun at shoulder level, points at the target and fires. Body position in the point-shoulder variation is the same as described earlier for the two-handed standing position, except the arms are held at shoulder level rather than at eye level and the shooter's eyes are focused on the target rather than the front sight. (See Figure 57.)

ONE-HANDED STANDING POSITION

Some self-defense situations may not allow you to use your second hand to support the gun. It is, therefore, advisable that you learn one-handed shooting. The one-handed standing position will have the following characteristics:

- **Position of Body** (See Figure 58)

  1. Body angled toward left or right target, depending on which hand you shoot with.
  2. Feet shoulder-width apart with body weight equally distributed.
  3. Shooting arm fully extended in front of face, with head erect.

- **Position of Handgun** (See Figure 59)

  1. Handgun is held with the shooting hand in alignment with the shooting eye.

- **Assuming the Position**

  1. Move to the firing point.
  2. Angle body toward target area, positioning feet appropriately.
  3. Attain the proper grip:
     a. With finger off trigger, hold the handgun in the

Figure 57.

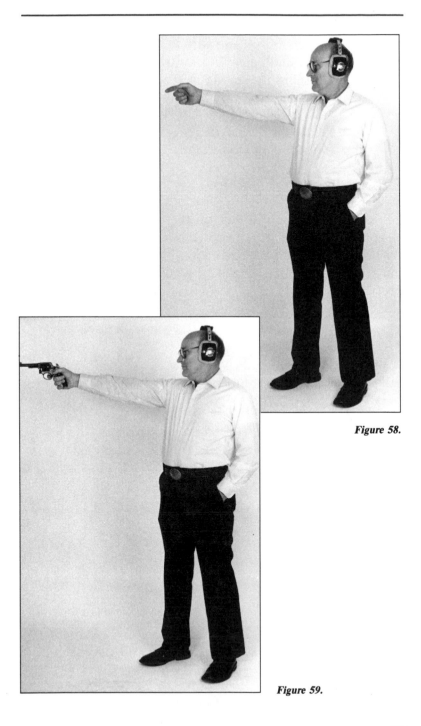

Figure 58.

Figure 59.

nonshooting hand with the handgun grip between the thumb and forefinger.

b. Pushing the handgun firmly to the rear of the shooting hand, wrap the lower three fingers around the grip.

4. Extend arm toward target area.

5. Align sights in front of the shooting eye.

Other Shooting Positions

Other handgun shooting positions, such as prone, kneeling, sitting and modifications on the standing position, may be equally effective for self-protection shooting. But, as with the positions which have been described in detail, these positions require practice to perfect and to maintain shooting proficiency.

PART II
CHAPTER 3
WORKBOOK REVIEW

What are common handgun shooting positions?

What is the distinguishing characteristic of the point-shoulder variation?

NOTES

4. MAINTAINING YOUR SKILLS

Practice

Shooting is like any other physical or mental skill. Your proficiency level depends on how often you practice. If you were a great golfer or tennis player in school, you practiced regularly to maintain skills. If you have not played in a few years, chances are you no longer perform as effectively. The same is true for shooting. After learning the fundamentals, you must practice regularly to maintain a reasonable level of proficiency.

The NRA Personal Protection Program is designed to give handgun owners basic safety and marksmanship skills. Each year, through this course, thousands of men and women from a wide variety of backgrounds develop confidence in their ability to handle handguns safely and to shoot accurately for the purpose of self-protection. Most of them discover that shooting can also be rewarding, relaxing, satisfying and fun.

You can build on your foundation of knowledge and skill by becoming involved in organized shooting activities. On the local, state and national levels, NRA-affiliated clubs offer a wide range of recreational and competitive handgun shooting activities — many geared for the beginning shooter.

As you develop skill and confidence, you will realize there is always something new to learn, and a new challenge to pursue. The NRA hopes that you will use your knowledge and skills for a lifetime of enjoyment from the shooting sports.

Qualification Shooting

An exciting way for shooters to improve their ability is through participation in NRA Qualification Programs, consisting of courses which allow you to advance at your own pace while rewarding you with certificates and brassards each step of the way. As your ability improves and you meet the criteria for one award level, you proceed to the next. Awards are presented for achievement at pro-marksman, marksman, sharpshooter, expert and distinguished expert skill levels.

Information on the new pistol qualification program is printed in the appendix of this handbook. Brochures describing

Figure 60. *NRA has a number of challenging and enjoyable handgun qualification programs.*

other qualification courses are available from the NRA Sales Department.

Training Opportunities

The quickest and most effective way to develop shooting skills is through expert instruction. NRA-affiliated clubs and other community groups across the nation offer NRA Basic Firearm Training Courses in:

- Pistol
- Rifle
- Shotgun
- Muzzleloading Pistol
- Muzzleloading Rifle
- Muzzleloading Shotgun
- Home Firearm Safety
- Personal Protection

The NRA Training Department can put you in touch with an NRA Certified Instructor in your area for course

Figure 61. *An NRA instructor can not only teach you the basics, but can also introduce you to recreational shooting opportunities in your community.*

information and offerings. In addition, the NRA offers a series of inexpensive books, films and tapes that describe and illustrate the fundamentals of shooting.

Leagues and Competitive Shooting

Many people discover that shooting can be a rewarding sport and that their marksmanship skills improve rapidly. Organized competitive shooting matches provide an excellent opportunity to refine these skills and to test them against others. The NRA establishes rules for shooting competitions, sanctions tournaments and maintains a computerized record system for all classified shooting competitors. For more information on competitive shooting, contact the NRA Competitions Division.

Practice With Your Friends

Throughout the United States, millions have joined or have organized shooting clubs to pursue their shooting interests. You, too, can become involved. There are more than 12,000 local NRA-affiliated shooting clubs, offering a variety of new shooting activities and social opportunities. Besides being places to

Figure 62. *Millions of Americans participate in recreational and competitive shooting programs annually.*

shoot, local clubs provide NRA Certified Instructors to help you develop your skills. You will have opportunities to participate in qualification programs and club competitions. The greatest benefit of membership in a local club is, of course, meeting others who share your interests in developing safety and marksmanship skills. For information on shooting clubs in your area, write to the NRA Clubs Department.

The National Rifle Association of America

Founded in 1871 and now three million members strong, the National Rifle Association is America's oldest sporting organization. The NRA is dedicated to the promotion of firearms safety and training, to the development of community service and to the preservation of the individual American citizen's right to keep and bear arms. Today, after maintaining these commitments for more than a century, the NRA is the nation's training leader in the firearms and shooting field.

NRA activities encompass virtually every element of the shooting world. Its programs range from activities in such specialized areas as gunsmithing and collecting, to broad-based involvement in the development of America's Olympic shooters. The NRA certifies instructors, affiliates clubs and sanctions tournaments and shooting championships in communities across America. It sets national standards for firearm safety, training and coaching, for shooting competition, for hunting and for a variety of firearms education opportunities. Members may participate in group insurance programs and other benefits. They receive monthly magazines filled with informative articles about shooting activities and events and they have access to an array of publications encompassing all the shooting and firearm interests. This book is but one of them.

Of all NRA activities and objectives, the most important is to protect and defend your constitutional right to own and to use firearms for all legitimate purposes, assuring that you will always be in a position to exercise your individual rights of self-preservation and defense of family and person.

Whatever your shooting interest, NRA encourages you to keep shooting, to continue improving and to stay involved in the growing family of American marksmen.

PART II
CHAPTER 4
WORKBOOK REVIEW

What are some ways to maintain and develop your shooting skills?

What is the difference between qualification shooting and competitive shooting?

How could you find a shooting range in your area?

NOTES

PART THREE:

BEING PREPARED

N R A

PERSONAL
PROTECTION
P R O G R A M

1. AVOIDING CRIMINAL ATTACK

While the NRA's expertise is firearm safety and marksmanship instruction, this chapter will provide information on a subject related to personal protection: how to avoid criminal attack. Although the following summary serves as a starting point for avoiding a violent confrontation, the NRA encourages you to learn more about this subject from local police or other community agencies. As a part of the NRA Personal Protection Course, this topic is taught by a local expert.

Home Security

A U.S. Department of Justice study (January 1985) reveals that a substantial proportion of violent crimes occur in the home during household burglaries. If you are at home when a criminal forcibly and illegally gains entry, you have one chance in three of becoming a victim of violence. Burglary has the potential to lead to far more serious crimes than does a property offense, since a burglar may inflict physical harm on household members during the commission of a crime.

Unlawful or forcible entry of a residence can be discouraged. Investing the time to make your home difficult to enter is important because burglars and other criminals look for easily accessible targets.

- **Locks:** A good home security plan starts with locked doors and windows. Why make your residence an easy target by having ineffective locks or by not using the locks you have? Doors should be solid wood or metal and have metal frames for heightened security. Deadbolt locks should be installed on all doors leading into your residence. Security chains are not reliable since chains can be pulled out of most door frames with only moderate force. Doors with glass should be covered with metal grillwork and ground-level windows should be secured with locks, jam-bars or nails through the window sashes.

    Locks must be *used* to be effective. The U.S. Department of Justice has found that burglary occurs more often in the warmer months, possibly because home-

Figure 63. *Locks are only useful if they are always used.*

owners create opportunities for easy entry by leaving doors and windows open. Locks should be used *at all times* since as many unlawful entries occur in the daytime as at night.

Upon moving into a new house or apartment, change the locks or have the tumblers reset. Never hide your key under a mat, flower pot or in other easily accessible places.

- **Around Your House or Apartment Building:** Lights in and around buildings discourage criminals. If you live in an apartment, make sure entries, hallways and elevators are brightly lighted and maintained by the management. Removing and breaking bulbs in such places are common tactics of criminals.

97

Never go into darkened areas alone. Either have a friend walk you to your door or call the building supervisor to replace the missing lights. Shrubbery around entrances and walks should be trimmed as they can provide criminals with hiding places.

At night in your home, draw your window shades or blinds, making sure they completely cover the windows to eliminate cracks for peeping toms or burglars casing future targets.

When working in your yard, attic, laundry room or any place away from your home's entry areas, lock all doors. While you are busy elsewhere, burglars could easily enter your home unnoticed.

When they are not in use, put away your lawnmower, tools, bikes and other valuable items and keep your garage or lawn shed doors locked. An open garage door not only makes items readily available to burglars, but can also offer a criminal easy access to your home.

Single women should use their first and middle initials and their last name—rather than their full name—on the mailbox and in the phone book.

Never tell a stranger that you are home alone or what hours you usually are away from home. All family members should be instructed to give no information to strangers on the telephone. Co-workers should be directed not to tell strangers when you are on vacation or on a business trip.

- **Strangers at Your Door:** Never open your door to a stranger. Wide-angle door viewers are an inexpensive aid for identifying people at your doorstep. Employees of utilities companies always carry identification, wear the proper uniforms and will wait outside while you call to verify their identity. If strangers ask to use your phone, offer to make the call while they wait outside. If someone claims to be delivering an item, have the package left by the door. REMEMBER: Never allow a stranger to enter your home.

Figure 64. *Be alert to strangers particularly when everything seems to be just right! That is precisely what a criminal wants you to think.*

Battery operated door and window alarms that make a loud noise can frighten off a potential intruder. They will also give you a warning of attempted illegal entry into your home. Many types of alarms are available to suit your particular needs.

- **On the Street:** To avoid criminal attack on the street, the following advice is offered by experts:
  - Avoid walking alone at night, especially in dark or poorly lighted areas.
  - Walk confidently, briskly and be alert to your surroundings.

- Park in well-lighted, accessible parking lots.
- Have your keys ready as you approach your car's front door.
- If you suspect you are being followed, cross to the other side of the street or go to an open business or home.
- Be suspicious of people loitering or "hanging around" the entrance to your apartment building. Avoid them.
- If you feel threatened or intimidated by the occupant of a car, turn and run in the opposite direction that the car is traveling and go to the nearest lighted building or home as quickly as possible.

Figure 65. *Under unusual circumstances, it is generally a good idea to have someone go with you or escort you to your car.*

- When driving, keep car doors locked and secure valuables and/or purse out of sight, on the floor or in the trunk.
- If your car breaks down in a remote area, raise the hood and tie a white cloth to the radio antenna or door handle. Then, get back into your car, lock the doors and wait until help arrives. Naturally, if your car has a CB radio, call for help on Channel 9.

Other situations in your home and business will, of course, require different preparations and reactions on your part.

- **Staying Alert:** Always be alert and aware of your surroundings and be determined to use whatever precautions are necessary to avoid becoming a victim. The following chapter contains information you may need if you have taken steps to avoid criminal attack, but such an attack is imminent. The last chapter surveys federal laws pertaining to handgun ownership and transportation.

PART III
CHAPTER 1
WORKBOOK REVIEW

List measures you can take to discourage criminal entry in *your* home.

What steps can you take to avoid criminal attack on the street?

What are some ruses a criminal may use to enter your home?

NOTES

2. CONTROLLING A VIOLENT CONFRONTATION

Handling a life-threatening situation involving a violent criminal attack requires an understanding of "real conditions" present during confrontations between armed citizens and violent criminals. The use of a firearm is not the only or final means of self-protection, but if a gun must be used, the armed citizen should understand the ramifications of using a firearm before, during and after the confrontation. The criterion for self-defense and the use of deadly force is to employ that amount of force necessary to meet and overcome the force being used against you. Your goal is to *stop* and to *control* a life-threatening situation.

What constitutes a weapon in a criminal attack situation? A gun, knife, large rock, board, pipe or anything that can be used to inflict grievous bodily harm or death against another can be classified as a weapon.

A Criminal in Your Home

Regardless of the steps you take to prevent someone from forcibly entering your home, illegal entries may occur. Plan your actions ahead of time so you will know what to do. Prepare for future emergencies now by reviewing the options that you and your family have. To avoid a successful criminal attack in your home:

Be prepared:
- Know the layout of your home and be familiar with all entrances.
- Plan an escape route for you and for family members.
- Identify the room most likely to be your "safe spot" and have a telephone installed. Keep a flashlight near the phone and the police telephone number easily available.
- If having a handgun is part of your master plan to avoid becoming a victim, know how it operates and how to use it.

If a stranger is detected in your home:
- **Keep your head.** By remaining calm, you will make

better use of the very short time you have to make critical decisions. Do not be complacent or deny that a criminal may be in your home.

- **Assess the situation.** Where do you think the criminal is located? Where are other persons in your home located? If armed self-defense is inadvisable or impossible, review in your mind the exits of your home. If there is an exit that you and your family can use to escape the criminal, leave as quickly and as quietly as possible. However, you are under no legal responsibility to leave your home.

- **Call the police.** Whether from your own home or from a neighbor's house, call the police. If you are in your home, inform the police of your location and the location of other family members. Always tell the police if

Figure 66. *When in doubt, NEVER HESITATE to call the police immediately. Most jurisdictions have a 911 emergency number.*

Figure 67. *Knowing the exact location of family members in the house is important during a criminal confrontation.*

you are armed. Also, attempt to determine if the police will respond in uniform or plain clothes so you can avoid a confrontation with the wrong person. Answer all questions as calmly as possible and don't hang up the phone until police arrive.

- **Go to a safe place.** Try to go to a predetermined "safe spot" with a phone where you will take your stand. In many cases, it will be a bedroom. Lock the door. If you hear someone outside the door, yell that the police are on their way. And, if you have a gun, tell the intruder that you are armed. Keep the police informed throughout the ordeal. NOTE: Never search your house if you suspect someone is there unlawfully. "Clearing a house" is dangerous and requires extensive training. Leave it to the police. Your efforts should be directed toward avoiding contact with the criminal.

- **Last Resort: Using Force.** Hopefully, you will never face a life-threatening situation wherein you are forced to make the "ultimate decision." If an attacker, heedless of your warnings that the police are coming and that you are armed, enters the room and presents a reasonable threat of deadly danger to you or your family, you will be in such a situation. If you have made the decision to own a handgun for self-protection, you should have already determined to use the gun as a last resort to protect innocent lives. If an attacker puts you in a position where you must use force, be sure to identify the attacker positively.

Conditions of a Confrontation Involving Deadly Physical Force

Most confrontations will occur quickly and at arm's length or within a confined space, such as a room, hallway or stairway. Actual distances vary and change rapidly during the confrontation, but usually remain quite close. The best defense is to attempt to maintain as much distance as possible between you and the criminal until the situation is under control.

Often there is a lot of movement by both the attacker and the armed citizen prior to and during a confrontation. The armed citizen must know this in advance and be careful to move in such a way that balance is maintained. It is also important that body movements remain versatile and flexible. There will be times when an attacker and the armed citizen are not on the same eye-to-eye level. This plays an important role in how the handgun is to be held so it can be used effectively and efficiently.

Most confrontations occur at night or in poor light. Therefore, while it is important to practice the fundamentals of marksmanship on a safe, well-lighted range, it is also desirable to practice in dim light, if possible.

In a home-defense situation, family members should be assigned specific functions to perform, such as staying in a certain room, calling the police and staying on the line. Knowing the specific location of family members will help you avoid mistaking them for the criminal.

Reaction vs. Action

The armed citizen must understand that his *reaction* time is slower than the *action* time of the criminal. Since the victim is often pre-selected by the criminal, the criminal has the advantage. The armed citizen, therefore, should do everything possible to avoid criminal attack by avoiding confrontation and by taking precautions in the home to discourage burglars. Yet, in spite of all actions taken to avoid criminal attack, a confrontation between an armed citizen and a criminal may be imminent. In such confrontations, the armed citizen must gain control of the situation to save his or her life.

During a high-stress situation, your body reacts in a number of predictable ways. When you are alarmed or excited, heart and pulse beat will become rapid, breathing becomes irregular; you may lose track of time, and you may notice a reduction in your ability to distinguish color or depth. Because these are normal reactions to stress, you should not be alarmed when these reactions occur during an armed confrontation.

Mental Conditioning and Thought Processes

Every person goes through a sequence of thought processes in preparation for, during and after a confrontation involving deadly force. An understanding of the various stages in this sequence will help the individual anticipate his own reactions and, thus, better control the situation.

1. **Complacency.** It always happens to the other person! This is perhaps the hardest stage to overcome in dealing with possible criminal activity. If one is complacent in his or her thinking, he or she will most likely become a crime victim. The armed citizen cannot REACT fast enough if he or she is complacent.

2. **Awareness.** This is the beginning of the thought processes in preparation for a potential confrontation. Citizens wishing to defend themselves should be aware of the proper selection of a firearm and ammunition and its storage and maintenance. They should know that, in addition to a gun, cover, concealment, shadows and poor light can be used as protection. What to say (if anything) prior to using a firearm in self-defense; at what point deadly physical force can be legally used and the manner in which to deal with investigative and/or judicial bodies after applying deadly physical force are to be considered. Awareness also involves the procedures of action of all household members as well as a pre-determined plan on the part of the armed citizen to have the perpetrator under CONTROL.

3. **Early Warning Sign of Danger.** This is, perhaps, the most sensitive period for the armed citizen and is crucial in establishing the armed citizen in CONTROL of the life-threatening situation. The armed citizen's holding of a handgun does not mean that he *must* fire it. Instead, the handgun is a tool used for CONTROL. That it is in the hands of an armed citizen should not indicate a DESIRE on the part of the citizen to use it, rather a WILLINGNESS to use it to defend one's life because of continued hostile and threatening behavior by the criminal.

4. **Imminent Use of the Handgun.** Life-threatening situations will escalate only by choice of the violent predatory criminal. The armed citizen should do everything possible to CONTROL THE SITUATION. Yet, jeopardy of the citizen is imminent when ability and means are available to the dangerous criminal to inflict harm. The armed citizen is now prepared to REACT to the violence being perpetrated against him or her.

5. **Actual Confrontation.** The armed citizen has no choice but to use that means of deadly physical force to meet

and to overcome the force being used against him or her. At this point, the armed citizen employs all the knowledge, skill and ability associated with the live firing of the handgun. The sole purpose of firing at this time is to STOP or to NEUTRALIZE the offender to save the life of the armed citizen.

If You Must Use Force

Using a means of force that may take a human life is not easy. Even armed citizens whose use of deadly physical force is totally justifiable find themselves racked with doubt. Post-shooting trauma can be extensive.

Citizens who use deadly physical force to protect their lives or the lives of loved ones can anticipate initial hostile reaction during the early phases of the police investigation. Law enforcement officers must determine if there was any criminal action on the part of the armed citizen and will immediately want a statement or an interview with the armed citizen. The citizen should *not* give any statement of any kind without an attorney present. Consult a lawyer as soon as possible.

Deadly Force and the Law

Exactly when are you legally permitted to use deadly force to protect yourself against criminal attacks? Laws regulating gun ownership and transportation differ greatly from area to area, as do laws concerning the use of deadly force for self-protection. While it is the responsibility of all firearms owners to be familiar with the laws in their city, county, and state, there are common elements of such laws.

Laws governing the use of force for self-protection are easily remembered by thinking of the acronym *JAM*. If you are in *JEOPARDY* of an attack (i.e., robbery, rape, felonious assault) by a criminal, and if the criminal has the *ABILITY* and the *MEANS* to inflict grievous bodily harm, you can use that amount of force necessary to meet and overcome the force being used by the criminal, thus stopping the attack and reestablishing your safety. Attackers have the MEANS when they possess a knife, a gun or other deadly weapons or instruments.

In some areas, homeowners may protect their property with force, while in others, only lives or limbs may be defended. However, deadly force may be used if absolutely necessary to stop or to resist rape or to prevent serious or grievous bodily harm or injury (with various meanings in different areas). "Deadly force" usually means any physical force calculated or likely to cause death or serious injury.

In some jurisdictions, you need not retreat before resorting to deadly force. In other jurisdictions, you have a duty to retreat if retreat may be accomplished with safety.

In general, the law is much more favorably disposed toward the use of deadly force in defense against predatory attacks (robbery, arson, home burglary, rape, felonious act, etc.) than in cases of defense during spontaneous disputes or brawls, such as those between acquaintances, relatives, party goers or automobile drivers involved in fights which escalate to physical force. There is no duty to retreat from the home when confronted by a predatory criminal, i.e., a criminal who is intent on rape, robbery, etc. in the home.

REMEMBER: It is the responsibility of the firearms owner to know and to observe all local, state and federal laws concerning gun ownership and use.

PART III
CHAPTER 2
WORKBOOK REVIEW

How would you prepare yourself to successfully avoid a criminal attack in your home?

What five points should you remember if a stranger is in your home?

1. _____
2. _____
3. _____
4. _____
5. _____

Why does the criminal generally have the advantage over an armed citizen during a criminal act?

How could firing conditions between an armed confrontation and a shooting range differ?

What are the five mental stages involved in a criminal confrontation?

1. _____

2. _____

3. _____

4. _____

5. _____

What does JAM mean?

NOTES

3. FIREARMS AND THE LAW

At the time this handbook was compiled, there were more than 20,000 federal, state and local laws and ordinances affecting the purchase, use, ownership, possession and transportation of firearms. Not only do laws vary greatly from one state to the next, but there are often major differences in the laws between counties and municipalities in the same state. The correct legal procedure in one area might be incorrect and illegal in another. You must learn the laws that are in effect in your area. Therefore, let us look at key points about the laws pertaining to firearms:

Ownership

* Federal law prohibits certain persons from owning or possessing firearms. Among those who *cannot* legally own or possess firearms are: (1) persons who have renounced their American citizenship; (2) individuals who have been dishonorably discharged from military service; (3) individuals who have been convicted of a felony; (4) narcotics addicts; (5) persons with certain types of mental illness or who have been committed to a mental institution or have been adjudicated mentally ill; and (6) illegal aliens (registered aliens can legally own firearms). In addition, persons under indictment may not ship or transport a firearm in interstate or foreign commerce or receive any firearm which has been shipped or transported in interstate or foreign commerce.
* Federal law provides for recordkeeping of firearm sales by licensed dealers. So, when purchasing a firearm, be prepared to provide the dealer with personal identification. The dealer will require you to sign a firearm acquisition form, certifying your age, birthplace and residence. You must also certify that you are not addicted to narcotics, under indictment, mentally ill and that you do not meet any of the other provisions that would prohibit you from owning or possessing firearms. Failure to provide accurate information is a federal felony.

Figure 68. *Be sure to know the laws pertaining to handguns. These are normally available from your law enforcement or prosecutors office. In addition, the NRA has available summaries of federal and state laws.*

- Some states and local jurisdictions require you to obtain a permit before purchasing firearms.
- Some states and local jurisdictions require the registration of firearms. Others require a specific waiting period between the time a firearm is purchased and the time it is delivered to you.
- Some .areas, such as Washington, D.C., have banned handgun ownership. In these areas, law-abiding individuals are denied their right to own a handgun for the protection of their lives or the lives of their families.

Transporting Firearms

Any time you transport a firearm, you are governed by federal, state and/or local regulations. For example:
- Many jurisdictions prohibit transporting a loaded firearm without a license to do so.

- Some state and local laws regulate how firearms can be transported. In many places, a license is required to carry a firearm openly or concealed in a vehicle. Generally, a firearm is considered to be "concealed in a vehicle" when it is covered from ordinary observation on the person or in such proximity as to be readily accessible to the occupants, such as in the glove compartment. As a precaution against uncertainty, firearms should be transported unloaded and locked in the trunk. Federal law allows you to transport — interstate — unloaded firearms in a trunk or a locked container, other than the glove compartment or console, regardless of state or local laws in the contrary, *if* you are allowed to transport or to carry the firearms at the point where your journey begins and at the point where your interstate journey ends. In some instances, you are required to transport a firearm in a case,

Figure 69. *Remember that in addition to federal laws, airlines can also establish their own regulations pertaining to the transportation of firearms. Be sure to check with them before you travel.*

shooting box or factory carton, which will also protect it from damage.

* Transporting a firearm on a commercial airline is subject to federal regulations. The firearm must be unloaded and placed in locked luggage or a locked gun container that is checked with the airline and put in the plane's baggage area. In addition, you must notify the airline that the firearm is in your luggage and must declare that it is unloaded. Some airlines have you pass through security clearance before checking your bags. Be sure to declare any guns you have in your bags *before* passing through security.

Naturally, any law is subject to change. Therefore, it is a good idea to contact a competent local attorney before purchasing a firearm or before attempting to transport one. Airlines and travel agents can give you the most up-to-date information about transporting a firearm aboard a plane. However, officials have sometimes been known to give incorrect information, resulting in the arrest of law-abiding gun owners. Check your source. Remember, ignorance of the law is never an excuse.

Carrying Firearms

* Many jurisdictions prohibit carrying a loaded firearm without a license.
* In many places, carrying a firearm openly or concealed on or about your person or in a purse requires a license.

PART III
CHAPTER 3
WORKBOOK REVIEW

Among those that federal law prohibits from owning or possessing a firearm are _mentally ill; addicts, etc._
To what must you attest when purchasing a firearm?

age
birthplace
Same (don't work @ Tecon.)

Summarize state and local regulations which may be enforced when you purchase a firearm.

Whom could you contact in your community for the specific laws pertaining to handgun ownership and use?

A competent local atty.
N.R.A. office

NOTES

POSTSCRIPT

Mastering the information provided in this handbook is only a preliminary step toward your becoming a responsible handgun owner. Information, instruction and guidelines are useful in theory, but the responsibility for safe, competent and legal application of knowledge and skill related to firearms *always* rests with *you*.

APPENDIX

NRA PISTOL MARKSMANSHIP QUALIFICATION PROGRAM

This qualification program is an excellent way to practice and improve your shooting ability. Firing may be done on a formal or informal range as long as it is safe. Awards include certificates, brassards and medals.

RULES

- Qualification awards must be earned in this order: Pro-Marksman, Marksman, Sharpshooter, Expert and Distinguished Expert.
- Qualification awards may be earned by anyone.
- Scores may be fired at any time, either in formal competition or in practice.
- Scores used to earn one award cannot be used again to earn another award.
- Any ammunition, either factory or handloaded, may be used.
- Any caliber handgun (centerfire or rimfire) may be used.
- Stages of firing are as follows:
  - Slow fire, which means that each shot must be fired within one minute.
  - Timed fire, which means that two five shot strings must be fired within 20 seconds each.
  - Rapid fire, which means that two five shot strings must be fired within 10 seconds each.
- Any timing device can be used to determine time duration in each stage.
- The following NRA Official Targets must be used as appropriate:
  - Slow fire — B2
  - Timed and rapid — B3
- Targets must be shot from 50 feet.

ORDERING INFORMATION

- Use NRA Standard Order Form to order items listed. Prices are subject to change without notice.

- Order forms and current prices are available from NRA Sales Dept., P.O. Box 5000, Kearneysville, WV 25430-5000, or call toll free (800) 336-7402. Hours: 9:00 a.m.–5:00 p.m. Eastern time.

Description	Item No.	Unit	Unit Price
Rifle and Pistol Qualification Course			
Brochure	EQ3N0050	each	NC
Brassard			
25 Foot Pistol	EQ5N0334	each	2.75
50 Foot Pistol	EQ5N0343	each	2.75
Brassard Rocker			
Pro-Marksman	EQ5N0407	each	1.25
Marksman	EQ5N0416	each	1.25
Certificate			
Pro-Marksman	EQ3N0103	each	NC
Marksman	EQ3N0112	each	NC
Medal			
50 Foot Pistol			
Pro-Marksman	EQ5N0941	each	3.25
Marksman	EQ5N0950	each	3.25
Outdoor Qualification Course			
Brochure	EQ3N1157	each	NC

Outdoor Qualification Course *(Continued)*

Brassard
Outdoor   EQ5N1306   each   3.25

Brassard Rocker
Marksman   EQ5N0416   each   1.25

Certificate
Marksman   EQ3N1255   each   NC

Collegiate Qualification Course

Brochure   EQ3N3253   each   NC

Brassard
Collegiate   EQ5N3402   each   3.25

Brassard Rocker
Marksman   EQ5N0416   each   1.25